Robots Everywhere!

Unpeeled by **Russ** and **Yammy**
with **Kelly Ang**
Illustrated by **Nicholas Liem** and **Alan Bay**

 **WS Education**

NEW JERSEY · LONDON · SINGAPORE · BEIJING · SHANGHAI · HONG KONG · TAIPEI · CHENNAI · TOKYO

Published by

WS Education, an imprint of
World Scientific Publishing Co. Pte. Ltd.
5 Toh Tuck Link, Singapore 596224
USA office: 27 Warren Street, Suite 401-402, Hackensack, NJ 07601
UK office: 57 Shelton Street, Covent Garden, London WC2H 9HE

National Library Board, Singapore Cataloguing in Publication Data
Name(s): Ang, Kelly. | Liem, Nicholas, illustrator. | Bay, Alan, illustrator.
Title: Robots everywhere! : unpeeled with Russ and Yammy / with Kelly Ang ;
    illustrated by Nicholas Liem and Alan Bay.
Other Title(s): Science everywhere! (WS Education)
Description: Singapore : WS Education, [2023]
Identifier(s): ISBN 978-981-12-3994-6 (hardcover) | 978-981-12-4046-1 (paperback) |
    978-981-12-3995-3 (ebook for institutions) | 978-981-12-3996-0 (ebook for individuals)
Subject(s): LCSH: Robots--Juvenile literature. | Robotics--Juvenile literature.
Classification: DDC 629.892--dc23

British Library Cataloguing-in-Publication Data
A catalogue record for this book is available from the British Library.

Desk Editor: Amanda Yun
Illustrators: Nicholas Liem & Alan Bay

Printed in Singapore

CONTENTS

Introduction 5

Guide 6
How to read this book

Chapter 1: 7
No such thing as working till you drop with these bots!

Chapter 2: 18
Is it a car? Is it a plane? Is it Superman? No, it's a robot!

Chapter 3: 35
Just call me Dr Bot

Chapter 4: 51
Do robot scientists dream of robots?

Chapter 5: 64
"You'll never have to mop your own floors again," they said...

Chapter 6: 78
It's not all work and no play!

Chapter 7: 92
Welcome to your future, kids: meet your robotic teachers!

Chapter 8: 106
They'll go where we cannot, to be our eyes, hands and feet

Chapter 9: 124
Robots of the future

A Guide to Experiencing Bonus Features in This Book

- QR codes will appear where there are Bonus Features.
- Scan the codes with a QR code scanner to access them!
- You will need access to the Internet/ WiFi to access the Bonus Features.

Before we begin, look out for these headers for a quick start to your journey with us!

Fact Snack

Get the low down on the most fascinating robot facts whenever you see this header – served with an extra dash of a-PEEL!

Let's scROOTinise!

With their out-of-this-world abilities, some robots are worth taking a closer look at! We'll tell you when you should whip out that magnifying glass to scROOTinise some of these tuber cool robots!

Spud the Bot

There are some really cool, really REAL robots doing what they do best in the world around you, if only you knew where to look! We'll help you spud these bots hard at work!

Chapter 1

No such thing as working till you drop with these bots!

Ever seen a robot hard at work? Scientists predicted that our world would be overtaken by robots by 2020, but it sure doesn't look that way yet, right? Except... You've probably met a robot but not even realised it!

Fact Snack

The word "robot" comes from the word "robota", which means "drudgery" (hard work) in the Czech language!

Are you picturing human-looking robots taking the place of people at work? Think again! Robots at work come in many different forms – from industrial arms to appliances on wheels. Of course, robots that look like us are in the works, but they're still some time away from being everywhere.

Here are some jobs they're doing great at so far!

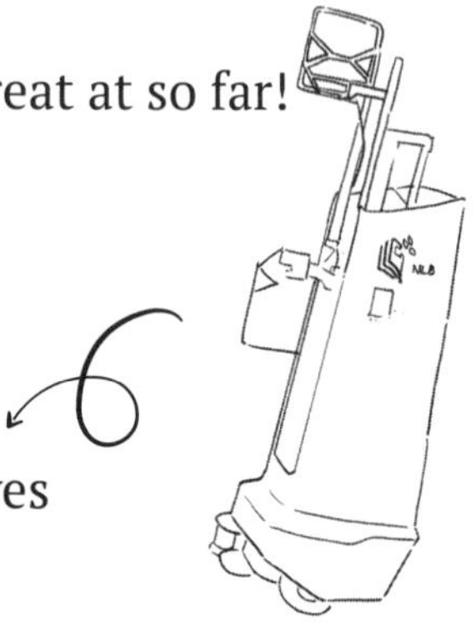

1. Manufacturing work in factories

2. Stocking of supermarket shelves

3. Arranging of books on library shelves

4. Packing shipment orders

5. Cleaning and disinfecting

6. Planting and harvesting crops

7. Call centre and customer service chats

Machines have been taking over jobs originally meant for people for a long time now. In the past, people had to make cloth over many days and weeks by hand-weaving threads. This changed when the Spinning Jenny was introduced in the 1700s. Instead of eight individual persons making eight pieces of cloth, the Spinning Jenny made it possible for one person to make eight pieces of cloth in the same amount of time! WOW!

Jobs that robots do well are mostly those that are repetitive and have a strong element of manual labour involved. That means we humans are freed up to do more things that require our amazing brains and creativity!

Fact Snack

Do you know which country has the most number of robots working at actual jobs? It's South Korea, with 932 robots for every 10,000 human workers in the country!

10,000 humans

932 robots

(According to the International Federation of Robotics 2021 World Robotics Statistics)

The factory: where robots first started to work

The very first jobs that robots did were in factories. In fact, industrial robots make up the bulk of robot workers in the world today. About 2.7 million robots are working in factories all over the world – that's about seven times the population of Iceland!

Fact Snack

Do you know what's the difference between a machine and a robot? While both machines and robots can carry out pre-set instructions efficiently, precisely and without getting tired, all robots are machines, but not all machines are robots! Machines aren't as clever as robots – they can't make any decisions for themselves whereas robots can. That's because robots have sensors that collect data about their environment, which they will use to make decisions.

To see when the first robot started working in a factory, we'll need to go back to the year 1961. Scan the QR code to have a look at the robot in action!

The Unimate is considered the world's first commercially used industrial robot. Although it was invented in 1954 by George Charles Devol — the man who is often called the "Father of Robotics" — it was only installed in a factory in 1961. Its first job? Die casting, handling and spot welding in a car assembly line in a General Motors factory!

It looks like a giant robotic arm, right?

It's a very efficient form for industrial robots to do what they need to do! Many industrial robots still look similar to this today.

If you can, you should definitely try to visit a factory to see an industrial robot at work. These robots make for an impressive sight since they work so swiftly and precisely. Most industrial robots look like robotic arms, much like how the very first industrial robot, the Unimate, looked like.

Today, they can do many things: from painting, to putting parts together, to packing and labelling. Some are able to do many things at one time, while others are specialised. Some of these arms are even collaborative and can learn new skills.

Spud the Bot

The largest arm robot in the world is the FANUC M-2000IA. It can carry loads of up to 2,300 kg. That means it can easily lift an entire car body! Thanks to its inbuilt machine vision sensors, this robot is great at handling materials with lots of care. It can even handle fragile materials like glass!

Hooray!!! This bot can easily lift 16,000 potatoes at a go. We're all set for potato world domination!

FANUC M-2000IA

2020: The year robots stepped up to help humans during the COVID-19 pandemic

2020 will be remembered as the year the world went into lockdown, thanks to COVID-19. For some of us, this meant spending our days hiding out at home, attending classes online, and having Mum and Dad work from home!

For people in government who run cities and countries, COVID-19 also meant needing to keep everyone safe. This meant keeping the environment clean and germ-free while also needing to ensure most people stay home. How did they solve this puzzle?

Robots, of course! With no need for social distancing (because have you ever heard of a robot catching a virus?), robots became the perfect solution during this period!

Spud the Bot

Supermarket robot Tally was hard at work stocking supermarket shelves in the United States in 2020. Its cameras and sensors help it to roam the shelves nimbly and avoid falling over anything in its way as it does its job. It was so speedy that it could check between 15,000 and 30,000 products an hour!

What trots on four legs, patrols the park without fear of the COVID-19 virus, and reminds people of safe distancing guidelines? That would be Spot the robotic pup! Spot has been available for industrial uses since 2019 but has since learnt new tricks thanks to COVID-19!

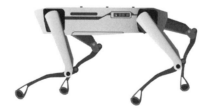

Spotlight on cleaning robots

There are all sorts of cleaning robots these days! From tray-clearing ones, to robots that go around sanitising public areas, to robots that can scale heights to wash the windows of skyscrapers – you'll be amazed at the variety of cleaning robots all around us.

With an increased need to keep places squeaky clean and germ-free, cleaning bots are in the spotlight these days! That's because they can sweep, mop, vacuum and disinfect tirelessly with no need for snack breaks (try doing that!), and are impervious to germs.

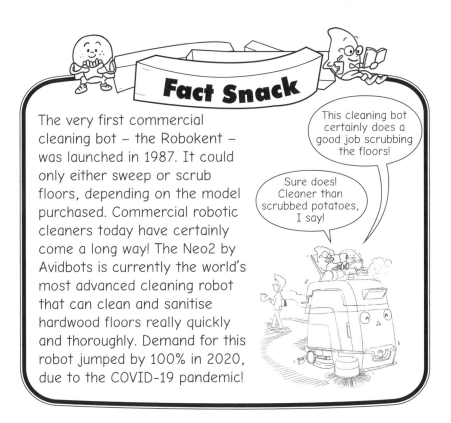

Fact Snack

The very first commercial cleaning bot – the Robokent – was launched in 1987. It could only either sweep or scrub floors, depending on the model purchased. Commercial robotic cleaners today have certainly come a long way! The Neo2 by Avidbots is currently the world's most advanced cleaning robot that can clean and sanitise hardwood floors really quickly and thoroughly. Demand for this robot jumped by 100% in 2020, due to the COVID-19 pandemic!

This cleaning bot certainly does a good job scrubbing the floors!

Sure does! Cleaner than scrubbed potatoes, I say!

Spud the Bot

Maintenance robots that inspect false ceilings, clean floors, disinfect lifts, and map mosquito density are now at work in a food centre in Singapore. The robots that inspect false ceilings will even be able to chase pigeons and mynahs away by emitting frequencies that only the birds can hear!

> Wait, why are we running from the pigeon-scaring robot when we're not pigeons?

> Who knows, let's just run before we're mashed!

Let's sCROOTinise!

Airports all around the world have welcomed impressive cleaning bots to their housekeeping teams! Cleaning robots that industriously scrub floors and kill bacteria with ultraviolet rays are currently roaming the terminals of Pittsburgh International Airport, London Heathrow, Singapore Changi Airport, Doha Airport, and Hong Kong International Airport. These autonomous cleaning bots do a really good job of cleaning: they scour the floors with high pressured water jets and added chemical disinfectants for an extra boost of squeaky clean. They're really smart too, and are equipped with sensors to map out their cleaning areas and avoid obstacles in their way. Neat, eh?

Tater Toons

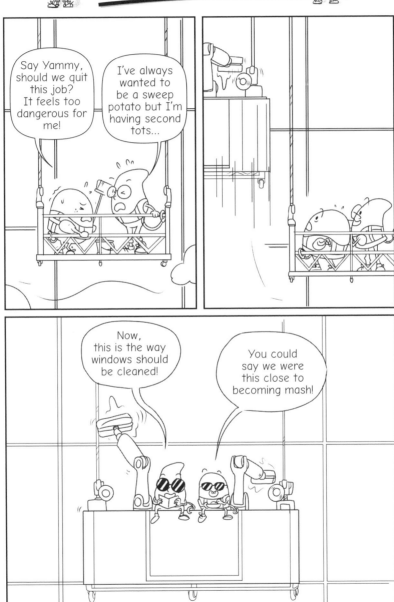

Chapter 2

Is it a car? Is it a plane? Is it Superman? No, it's a robot!

Vehicles that can drive themselves?

Vehicles that can take you anywhere you wish without needing a person around to operate them? Robotic vehicles have to be some of the coolest robots you could imagine! And people have been imagining them for years and years now. In fact, futurists (people who try to predict the future) thought that we'd be going around in automated, driverless vehicles by now already!

We're actually not too far off from reaching this goal! What if we told you that some trains are already operating autonomously without needing a driver? Or that automated drones have been on search and rescue teams when people are lost at sea? Surprised? Don't be!

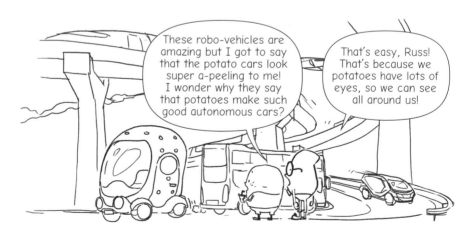

So just how far away are we from being able to sit in driverless cars to get around the city? No one knows for sure, but let's find out more about some cool robotic vehicles that you could easily meet someday on a road near you.

Fact Snack

The very first operational semi-automated car was developed in 1977, in Japan. It was a test model that could only run on specially marked streets, with sensors in the form of two cameras on its body and an analogue computer to control it. It could only move at a maximum speed of 30 km/h – that's about as fast as a bicycle!

It was able to navigate the street without a driver as it could track the white street markers with its machine vision.

You'll never catch me getting a ticket for speeding!

Robots on land – cars and buses

News flash! Scientists have come up with cars and buses that can drive themselves pretty well now. So, why aren't there more of these cool vehicles on our roads today? The answer is that many of these vehicles are still being tested in controlled environments so that we can be sure that these smart vehicles are safe for us to ride around in.

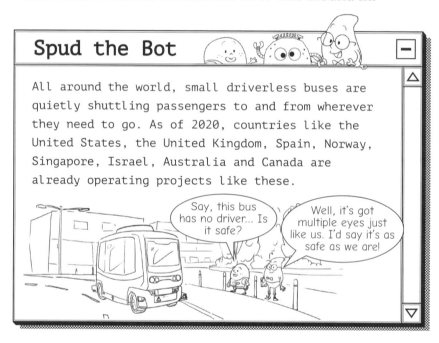

Spud the Bot

All around the world, small driverless buses are quietly shuttling passengers to and from wherever they need to go. As of 2020, countries like the United States, the United Kingdom, Spain, Norway, Singapore, Israel, Australia and Canada are already operating projects like these.

Say, this bus has no driver... Is it safe?

Well, it's got multiple eyes just like us. I'd say it's as safe as we are!

Scan the QR code to see this shuttle on the move in Singapore.

When it comes to autonomous vehicles, there are five levels of automation:

Level 0:	No Automation
Level 1:	Driver Assistance
Level 2:	Partial Automation
Level 3:	Conditional Automation
Level 4:	High Automation
Level 5:	Full Automation

Most robotic cars that exist today are at Level 3. These cars can drive themselves but only under precise road conditions and with fixed speed limits. And they still require a driver behind the wheel although he doesn't actually have to drive! The driver will only have to take over when the road conditions are not ideal. The big question on everyone's lips these days is: how many more years will it take to get to Level 5?

Robots on land – trains

Driverless trains are actually a standard feature in many train networks all over the world today. That's right, you could have been riding on a robotic train all this time without even realising it! That's because robo-trains have been running in many cities for many years now.

Fact Snack

The very first automatic railway system started running in 1968, in London. The Victoria line was the world's first driverless passenger train using the Automatic Train Operation (ATO) system, though it still ran with a driver in the cabin as a safety precaution.

Today, many trains still operate on the ATO system! There are four different levels of automation, known as Grades of Automation (GoA).

GoA 1: Everything is done manually; the train is driven by a driver and the doors are opened and closed by attendants

GoA 2: Train driving is partially automated, but there is still a driver in the cabin and attendants in the train

GoA 3: The train is driverless, with attendants in the train

GoA 4: The train is completely automated, with no staff onboard the train

Fact Snack

As of 2018, there are 64 fully automated train lines that run in 42 cities around the world. Over 50 percent of them are in Asia![1] Currently, the longest automated metro system in the world is in Singapore, with all 199 km of its Mass Rapid Transit lines achieving GoA 4.

[1] According to the International Association of Public Transport, March 2018 - https://www.uitp.org/publications/world-report-on-metro-automation/

Spud the Bot

China is the world's largest producers of potatoes and it is also home to the smartest rail network in the world. This 174 km route runs between the cities of Beijing and Zhangjiakou, with 10 stations in total. What's especially cool about this line is that every station is served by smart robots that will help passengers to check-in, carry their luggage, and give directions when asked. The trains are super smart too, with 5G touchscreen control panels at the seats, intelligent lighting, and lots of real-time safety sensors to monitor conditions in and out of the train.

Hi robot! How do I get to the nearest potato farm from this station?

Robots in the air

Ever heard your mum tell you that the sky's the limit? Roboticists sure think that way because robotic flying vehicles are coming right up! Many commercial airlines already rely on smart autopilot systems that take over when airplanes reach cruise mode. While going completely pilot-less on your next jet-setting holiday with your family may not be on the cards right now, there are already fully automated air taxis that run short, fixed routes for small numbers of people. You could even sit in one if you were in the right city!

Spud the Bot

The Volocopter, a smart drone helicopter that originated in Cologne, Germany, may be the next taxi service coming to a Southeast Asian city near you. If you're living in Singapore, you may be the first in the world to enjoy this service in the years to come! The company has signed a memorandum of understanding with ride-hailing app Grab to explore the setting up of an air taxi service in suitable Southeast Asian cities. The aim? To ferry 10,000 passengers a day in a busy, bustling city. Would YOU like to sit in one?

The very first gyroscopic autopilot, affectionately known as George, was invented just nine years after the Wright brothers took flight by a man named Lawrence Sperry. George helped planes to automatically balance during flight so that the pilot would not have to frantically push and pull levers like Wilbur Wright did.

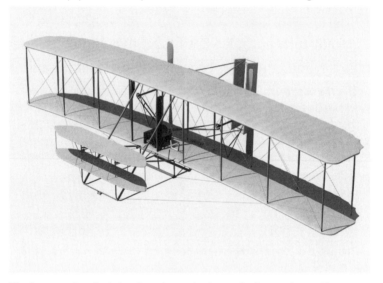

Today, autopilot technology is largely based on the computer-run fly-by-wire autopilot system, which was introduced by aerospace company Boeing in the late 1980s. This autopilot system is so clever that it can interpret the pilot's intention based on his action and execute it in the safest and smoothest way possible. This is why most planes are flying on autopilot mode about 80–90% of the total flight time!

Let's sC**ROOT**inise!

Modern autopilot systems are really clever, but commercial passenger planes still require two well-trained pilots onboard at all times. That's because the system still cannot make its own decisions without human input. So, what CAN the autopilot system do? Well, its main job is to keep the aircraft on a set course at cruising altitudes, and that already takes a lot of work off human pilots. Imagine having to manually keep the plane at a fixed speed and altitude for hours and hours on end! It's an awful lot of work. Truly autonomous planes are not that far away from reality though. Aerospace company Airbus managed to successfully test a fully automated take-off on one of its newest aircraft, the Airbus A350-1000 XWB, from the Toulouse-Blagnac Airport in France. This was achieved with cameras on the plane's body that were fitted with special technology to help it recognise the runway, so that it could keep a straight path when taking off. It could even make its own adjustments when faced with debris or wind, without the need for pilot intervention!

While commercial planes may take a little while more to become 100 percent self-flying – not because the technology does not exist but because people still feel safer with a fellow human being onboard to man the plane – small loads of cargo could be flown on pilotless planes very soon.

Spud the Bot

Meet the small but very smart aircraft that may be the first in the world to self-fly commercially – the Cessna 208 Caravan turboprop. Logistics company FedEx has tied up with robotics start-up Reliable Robotics to potentially use these small autonomous planes to transport cargo to remote areas. The Cessna 208 Caravan has demonstrated that it can fly and land fully autonomously. That's no mean feat, considering most planes still need pilots to help them land! What's helping it to fly solo is a super smart platform that can be used on any fixed-wing aircraft. This system includes avionics, software, mechanisms, a communications system, remote control interfaces, and a backup system for a pilot on the ground to take over if needed. Right now, a pilot still helps it to manage extreme weather conditions or air traffic from a control centre on the ground.

Scan the QR code to have a look at a Cessna flying without a pilot in its cockpit!

Another type of flying plane-bots are drones. Yeah, those really cool remote-controlled planes that are fun to fly! Did you know that there are now **self-flying** drones that you can get your hands on? Time to pop open that pack of potato chips and watch your drones fly!

Spud the Bot

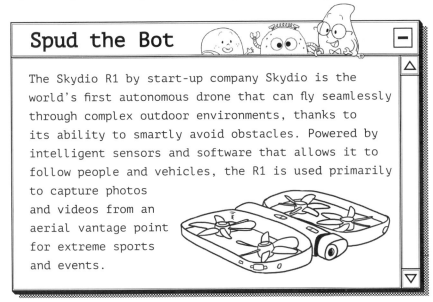

The Skydio R1 by start-up company Skydio is the world's first autonomous drone that can fly seamlessly through complex outdoor environments, thanks to its ability to smartly avoid obstacles. Powered by intelligent sensors and software that allows it to follow people and vehicles, the R1 is used primarily to capture photos and videos from an aerial vantage point for extreme sports and events.

Robots in the water

You've seen robots on land and robots in the air, now it's time to check out some robots in the oceans and seas. There are two main types of maritime robots: Unmanned Surface Vehicles and Autonomous Underwater Vehicles.

Fact Snack

Unmanned Surface Vehicles are ships and boats that can navigate their routes autonomously without the need for human intervention. They're great at avoiding collisions and finding the most efficient routes for a voyage.

Autonomous Underwater Vehicles are robots that can travel autonomously underwater, and there're so many of them these days in many shapes and sizes. One of the main uses of these underwater bots today is the studying and mapping the floors of water bodies, and deep-sea exploration. As technology evolves, the way these robots look are starting to change too – from clunky, heavy-duty submarines to sleek animal-like bots. Maybe one day, we'll even get to see a potato robot that dives deep into the sea...

Scan the QR code to have a look at how a MantaDroid, an autonomous underwater vehicle, looks almost like an actual manta ray as it swims!

Spud the Bot

If you see a humanoid-looking bot swimming among the corals the next time you go scuba-diving, it's probably the Ocean One robot. Developed by Stanford Robotics Lab, this underwater robot is equipped with two fully articulated arms that are dexterous enough to handle archaeological artefacts and has sophisticated force sensors to replicate the sense of touch* for its pilot. It also has stereoscopic vision that allows the pilot to perceive depth. This means that its pilot can almost see and feel exactly what the robot is experiencing in real time! Since it was introduced in 2016, this robot has been deployed to explore the shipwreck of La Lune off the southern coast of France and investigate underwater volcanic structures in Santorini, Greece.

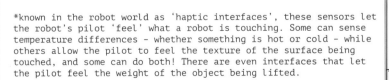

*known in the robot world as 'haptic interfaces', these sensors let the robot's pilot 'feel' what a robot is touching. Some can sense temperature differences - whether something is hot or cold - while others allow the pilot to feel the texture of the surface being touched, and some can do both! There are even interfaces that let the pilot feel the weight of the object being lifted.

Let's sC**ROOT**inise!

Many animals and plants in nature are so smartly designed that you'd be amazed. For instance, did you know that manta rays have perfected the art of efficient swimming? They're such graceful swimmers, cruising through turbulent waters with ease by effortlessly flapping their pectoral fins. Roboticists from the National University of Singapore have created a robot that mimics the efficiency of the manta ray by recreating the way manta rays propel themselves forward as they flap their fins to drive water back. Named the MantaDroid, it can swim for up to 10 hours at a top speed of approximately 2.5 kilometres per hour, powered only by a single electric motor on each fin. This helps the MantaDroid navigate through aquatic plants without getting tangled up — a big benefit in search and rescue operations! Engineers spent two years testing out 40 different fin designs to get the fin design of the MantaDroid just right. Yukon (You can) say it was TOT-ally a labour of love!

Some people may say that it's easier to fully automate a boat than a car. After all, the seas and oceans are largely vast expanses of open water with less things that boats could collide with. The main challenge that autonomous ships face is being able to stand up to monster storms at sea, where the waves can go up to three metres high on average. So, for a start, robo-boats are setting sail from calm, inland waters, where the route is simple and there isn't much traffic.

Spud the Bot

In 2018, the world got to have a look at the first fully automated ferry, named the Falco, which sailed between Parainen and Nauvo in Finland. Developed by automobile maker Rolls-Royce and Finnish state-owned ferry operator Finferries, the Falco successfully ferried 80 invited guests across the 1,664-metre route without any intervention from the crew. Equipped with sensors and an AI system that allow it to build a detailed picture of its surroundings in real time and alter its course and speed when necessary, the Falco was able to avoid collisions in its path and berth autonomously.

Fact Snack

While autonomous boats and ships are relatively young, autonomous underwater vehicles have been around for quite a bit longer. The very first underwater bot was the Self-Propelling Underwater Research Vehicle developed in 1957 by scientists from the University of Washington. It was used primarily for data-gathering, and it could operate for four hours and dive to depths of 10,000 feet!

Tater Toons

Yammy and Russ are on a mission to deliver a box of oysters from the UK to Belgium onboard the robotic sea vessel, **the Sea Kit Maxlimer.** The route will take it through a busy passage in the North Sea. It has been more than 15 hours since it left West Mersea, UK.

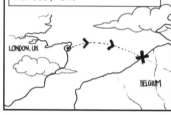

LONDON, UK

BELGIUM

Are you abso-root-ly sure we don't need to do any steering on this vessel, Yammy? It feels like a really long time since we left land. Could we be lost?

I-daho (I dunno), Russ... My eyes are so heavy, I can't keep them peeled open...

ZZzzzz...

Belgian city of Ostend

See, didn't I tell you to just relax?

It sure isn't easy to get used to the idea of a robo-boat that's smart enough to navigate its own ROOTS (routes) without a crew to manage it all...

Chill out, Russ! Let's bring along some potato chips for our next robotic boat ride so we can really kick back and relax!

Chapter 3

Just call me Dr Bot

When robots first started helping in surgery

You're wheeled into the operating theatre, expecting to see the friendly face of your surgeon looking at you, but what greets you first is a... stainless steel robot? It's already happening in a few countries for specific surgeries.

For now, robot surgeons aren't left to carry out entire procedures by themselves, so you don't have to fear rogue robots sawing you up with wild abandon. (Can we all say THANK GOODNESS?) Human surgeons still oversee the surgery, control the robotic arms remotely, or step in to take over where needed.

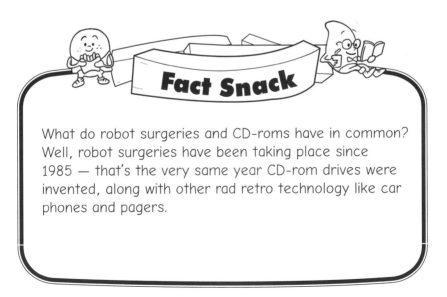

Fact Snack

What do robot surgeries and CD-roms have in common? Well, robot surgeries have been taking place since 1985 — that's the very same year CD-rom drives were invented, along with other rad retro technology like car phones and pagers.

Robots have been assisting us in these kinds of surgeries for quite a bit now:

- Heart bypass and valve repair
- Tumour removal, especially in the brain
- Kidney transplant
- Knee and hip replacements
- Spinal surgery
- Retina and eye procedures

Since 1985, more than 3 million robot-assisted procedures have been carried out!

A closer look at cool surgical robots!

All humans get tired. Yes, even video-game-and-television-loving little girls and boys like you. One of the biggest plus points of surgical robots is that they don't tire out or lose focus during longer operations! They are also able to operate with greater precision, if they are fed the correct information.

There are currently a few types of robotic surgeons out there, and most of them function in about the same way: surgeons pre-programme a multi-armed robot to carry out the procedures and monitor the surgery from 3D screens.

Spud the Bot

The Da Vinci Surgical System is a really high-tech surgical robot that is currently being used in 56 different countries. With the help of the Da Vinci, surgeons are able to make smaller incisions with greater precision as the robotic hands are able to twist and rotate at a greater degree than a human hand. The arms can be fitted with tiny surgical tools such as forceps, clamps and cutting tools, which can be moved to a fraction of a millimetre - that's basically smaller than a full-stop!

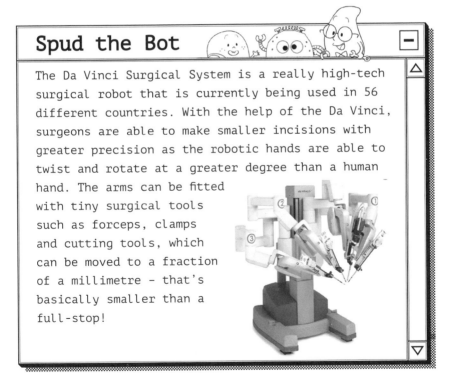

If the Da Vinci is so awesome, why aren't more hospitals using it? Well, its high price is one big reason – it actually costs about US$2 million per bot! Good thing there are other surgical bots today that have been developed for specific types of surgeries to help doctors. Let's have a look!

Fact Snack

1. In China, the Micro Hand S. is being developed and tested for laparoscopic surgery by Tianjin University. Other than its dexterous mechanical arm that can freely rotate 360 degrees around, it is also equipped with a super camera that gives surgeons up to 10 times more detail than the human eye can naturally see.

2. In Japan, the EMARO robot-assisted surgery platform lets surgeons have hands-free control while monitoring readings and data from other devices. The three movable cameras also give surgeons a much clearer look inside a patient's body.

Let's sCROOTinise!

Surgical robots today aren't exactly 100% autonomous yet because of the BIG question of who takes responsibility if something goes horribly wrong on the operating table. So roboticists are working on developing surgical robots to be the best assistants a doctor could need or want! Most surgical robot systems are made up of nimble mechanical arms, a sophisticated camera, and a console system that gives the surgeon a detailed overview of the entire process.

Automated Needle Targeting System by NDR Medical

Meet the Automated Needle Targeting (ANT) System, a fancy sounding robot that has been quietly helping surgeons and other doctors with surgeries and procedures that are not overly invasive. Also known as your newest AI-powered surgeon!

It was developed in 2015 by Alan Goh and Dr

Jason Ng of NDR Medical Technology, specifically because there wasn't such a robot doing this job before they created it. What does it do? In a nutshell, it's an image-guided robot that helps position a needle

Photo credit: NDR Medical.

precisely for a procedure. It also decides how deeply the needle should be inserted without the need for human guesswork or estimation.

The ANT has been tested in clinical trials in countries in Asia including Malaysia, China and Japan, and has received approval to perform kidney stones procedures in Europe, Singapore and Malaysia. It's certainly set to change the way simple operations are done, one automated needle at a time!

Curious to see how the ANT looks like up close?
Let's have a good look!

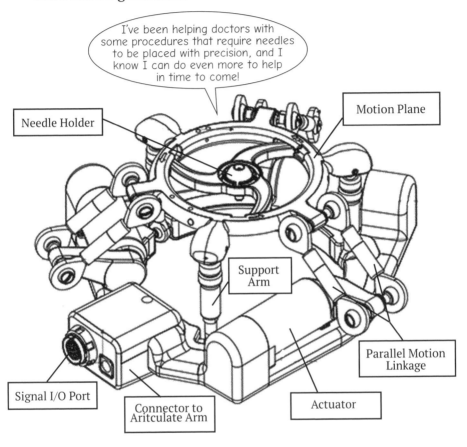

I've been helping doctors with some procedures that require needles to be placed with precision, and I know I can do even more to help in time to come!

Needle Holder

Motion Plane

Support Arm

Parallel Motion Linkage

Signal I/O Port

Connector to Aritculate Arm

Actuator

Scan the QR code to have a look at the ANT in action!

Spud the Bot

If this AI surgical assistant sounds like it's the smartest kid in the operating theatre, we agree with you! Alan Goh shares three cool things about the ANT that not many people know:

1. It works like the Google maps of your body, thanks to its precise imaging that allows doctors to see exactly where the needle will be placed before it goes in. The system allows surgeons and doctors to see and assess tumours and lesions in real time too, so diagnoses are even quicker than before.

2. You don't need to be a super experienced doctor or clinician to use this robot! Doctors, clinicians and other medical practitioners can use this smart little bot easily with just some simple training, guiding the needle to where it needs to go with a press of a few buttons and its smart AI imaging system. Wow!

3. It's been used for a number of procedures now, including simple surgeries and biopsies of the lungs and kidney.

Tiny and mighty: nanobots

You probably already know that size is not all that matters. In fact, sometimes, the tiniest things hold the biggest surprises. Some of the most amazing medical robots being developed today are miniscule nanobots that are even tinier than the dot of the exclamation mark at the end of this sentence! There still aren't any nanobots being used for actual treatments or procedures, but we're getting there soon.

Let's scROOTinise!

Nanobots don't quite look like your typical robot. Many of them look like medicine pills or may have soft bodies that crawl or swim through your body. They're mostly made of microscopic DNA or nano-particles. They're also sooooooo tiny that they don't even need a battery or power source to run; our human body heat is enough to keep them running!

Nanobots have great potential in treating cancers and other illnesses. We meant it when we said the smallest things often hide the biggest surprises!

The telemed doctor will see you now!

Feeling too yucky to crawl out of bed to see your doctor in the clinic? You'll be glad for telemedicine robots for sure! These bots that do simple and routine diagnostics and provide remote consultations with doctors have been around for a while now, but their use remained limited – until the COVID-19 pandemic struck.

It may seem like a relatively uncomplicated thing to take a patient's heart rate and temperature, but such robots reduce the spread of viruses and germs, which is very helpful indeed.

Fact Snack

Did you know that the very first idea of telemedicine was raised way back in 1925? An American inventor envisioned the use of the "teledactyl". Nope, that's not a dinosaur. It's a device that would let doctors speak to their patients through a screen and touch them with spindly robotic arms. Fast forward almost 100 years later and his dream seems like it could become reality, couldn't it?

Nope, not a pterodactyl, but a teledactyl!

Let's sC**ROOT**inise!

The first telemedicine robot – the RP-Vita – made its debut in 2013 in the United States. It is a cloud-based robot that's extremely easy to use: you only need to know how to operate a tablet to be able to use the RP-Vita! It can be connected to ultrasound imaging machines, digital stethoscopes and other advanced medical diagnostic equipment, so that doctors and nurses can access important diagnostic data to treat patients even if they're not physically there.

Scan the QR code to have a look at the RP-Vita at work in a hospital!

Nursing care robots

For the first time ever in world history, there are more people over the age of 65 than young people under the age of 5. And older folks need more medical care – it's just a fact of life. This means that the demand for nursing care for elderly folks will only continue to grow and grow and grow... So all we can say is, thank ROOTNESS for nursing care robots!

Fact Snack

Just like human nurses, nursing robots need to be able to do lots of things! Other than helping to measure a patient's heart rate and blood pressure, they also need to be able to help lift and turn patients in bed, assist them in walking or sitting, and even provide social care and therapy. As of 2020, more than 5,000 nursing institutions in Japan alone are using nursing robots to help human nurses care for their patients.

Meet some nursing robots such as Robear, Pepper and Paro.

1. Robear is a bear-type robot that has been working in old aged homes in Japan to help physically lift, turn and assist patients in walking.

2. Pepper is a humanoid robot assistant that helps guide the elderly folks in exercise routines, plays games and also holds simple conversations with the residents.

3. Paro is a furry seal robot that cares for patients with dementia by encouraging them to interact with it as a form of therapy. Paro reacts to a patient's touch and speech by moving its head, blinking its eyes and crying.

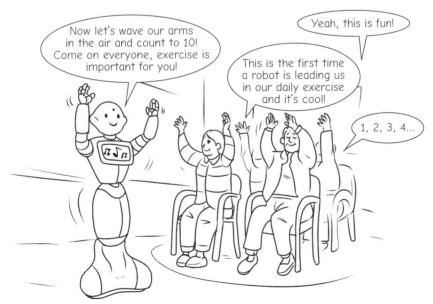

Who runs the pharmacies? BOTS!

The Royal Pharmaceutical Society has found that 72 percent of pharmacists in the UK are stressed. After all, they dispense more than 1 billion packs of medicine in a year! Dispensing those tiny pills all day and all night can really scramble your eyes and brain...

It's important to get it exactly right because dispensing the wrong medicines could make a patient reeeeeaaallly sick. Pharmacy robots are super precise, so pharmacists that have them around to help have a lesser chance of making mistakes.

Fact Snack

Machines that count pills have been around since 1971, and they've only been getting better and fancier since. As of 2010, there are more than 30,000 tablet counters being used in 35 countries all over the world! Today, pharmacy robots can automate up to 80 percent of a pharmacy's medicine dispensing. One such robot being used in many pharmacies today is the Parata Max 2, which looks like a cabinet with many drawers. It can fill, label and cap vials of medicine with NO human error at all! Human pharmacists still ultimately do a final check to ensure that everything is in good order but one day, perhaps there will be a robot to do this too.

Scan the QR code to see a pharmacy robot counting and packing pills without breaking a sweat.

Let's sC**ROOT**inise!

One of the most advanced robotic pharmacies in the world today is located in Stanford Health Care in the United States. It's got the whole process of dispensing medicine automated – from placing orders with the medicine makers, all the way to delivery straight to the patient in the hospital. Here, the bots and systems work to make this pharmacy so SPUD-TACULARLY robotic! Check out their process:

1.   The Swisslog BoxPicker stores ALL the medicines in the pharmacy in stacks of drawers. A mechanical picking robot moves up and down the aisles of the BoxPicker to pick out the boxes of medication needed. Every cannister and vial that's taken out is noted down so that the smart computer can remember exactly what's left on the shelves.

2.   The Swisslog PillPick bot packages a day's worth of medicine for individual patients. It can package up to 1000 doses in one hour. This used to be a job that took human pharmacists four to five hours to complete by hand!

3. These robots are also connected to the hospital's overall electronic medical record system to keep track of the medicines that are dispensed and place orders to replace what has been used. Doctors can also directly input medication orders for their patients into this system so that the pharmacy robots can get to work to pack the medicine requested for.

4. The medicines are delivered by the hospital's snazzy pneumatic tube delivery system directly to the patient's floor!

Chapter 4

Do robot scientists dream of robots?

Have you wondered what robot scientists dream of at night, given that they are the ones who create these robots that amaze us and make our lives easier? Do they dream of even more awesome robots in their sleep? Turns out, robot scientists don't dream of robots at night. Not all the time, anyway.

But they do think about robots a LOT. In almost all of their waking hours.

And according to Professor Marcelo Ang Jr, he's thought about robots for a long time now. Almost 40 years and counting, in fact. Wow!

Professor Ang is a robot scientist who was born in the Philippines. He teaches university students in Singapore and he hopes that someday, they will invent robots of their very own.

And, needless to say, he really loves robots.

"They're so cool!" Professor Ang exclaims with glee. "They solve problems for us and make our lives easier."

His interest in robots began way back, when he was working at Intel in Manila after graduating from university.

Professor Ang recounts with a glint in his eye, "I owned one of the very first IBM PCs in the 1980s, back when they were huge and bulky and nowhere near as powerful as the computers we have now."

He continues, "But to me, that IBM PC was amazing. It opened my eyes to the possibilities of how computers can make life so much easier for people. I was hooked."

Professor Ang's fascination with robots is still infectious today, and he shares his love for robots with his students at the National University of Singapore's Advanced Robotics Centre.

If you've never been there before, that's alright.

What you need to know is: it is here at this super special robot lab where Professor Ang spends a lot of his time researching robots. Very awesome, very cool robots like autonomous self-driving vehicles, personal assistant robots and climbing robots. He also researches functional but important robots, like robotic arms and robotic wheels and legs!

Fact Snack

Some special robots, like this self-driving bus here, have been made in the very lab that Professor Ang calls his second home.

I may not have a driver driving me, but I'm pretty sure my software drivers are 100% up-to-date!

The perfect robot

Out of all the robots he's worked on, does Professor Ang have a dream robot? Yes!

"I'd really love to have a personal assistant robot that helps me with my daily tasks. Not a scary, imposing one that looks like it can crush me, for sure. Even better if it can talk to me, entertain me, be my friend and teach me new things too!" Professor Ang chuckles.

It certainly makes sense for Professor Ang to want a friendly personal assistant robot to help him, given that he does so much in a single day. He teaches students, writes papers, studies how he can improve robots, and even dreams up new ones!

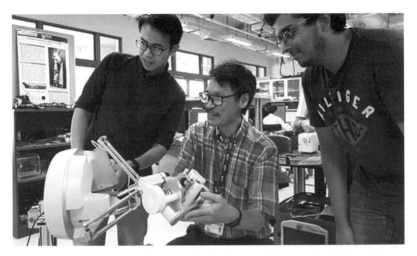

All in a day's work! Professor Ang is always doing something with his robots and students. No wonder he needs some help organising his schedule!

Photo credit: NUS Advanced Robotics Centre

(How much work do YOU get done in a day? We bet just completing your homework or some of your household chores would make Mum and Dad extremely pleased.)

"You know how emails and social media messages can get overwhelming to respond to, especially in the midst of all the other tasks on our to-do lists every day? Sometimes, they get buried under everything else," he adds with a resigned sigh. "So I hope that there will someday be a friendly-looking robot that can summarise all my emails and social media notifications, so that I can respond to them in an organised and timely manner."

Spud the Bot

Amazon has just launched Astro, its home personal assistant robot powered by its very clever AI, Alexa. (Yes, the same Alexa that can tell you if it will rain this evening, or the price of a carton of milk.) Can it summarise our emails and respond to them for us, like what Professor Ang hopes for? Not quite yet, but it's got great potential.

For now, it can map out your home and go to specific rooms on command, recognise faces and even deliver items to people in the house (amazing, considering it doesn't have hands). Astro can also roam your home keeping an eye on everything, play music on command and tell you if you've got plans for the day.

It doesn't look super human-like though, lacking arms and legs - it's actually a tablet screen with a digital face on wheels. Its creators say it's been made this way to gain trust so that more people feel comfortable using it. We have to say, it looks pretty friendly and helpful!

Watch Astro in action by scanning the QR code.

The problem with life-like robots

You may be surprised to hear this, but the greatest barrier to a life-like robot being made isn't the technology itself. It's actually people's attitudes towards such humanoid robots.

Professor Ang explains, "We humans may be uncomfortable with robots who look like us, talk like us, or act like us. It's a bit unnerving because you start to question what makes us human."

"Furthermore, there is the larger question of who takes responsibility for problems caused by the robot? Is it the owner or creator of the robot? Or is it the robot itself, since it's so life-like?" Professor Ang muses. "So up till now, humanoid robots that look extremely life-like haven't been available in the mass market."

Tater Toons

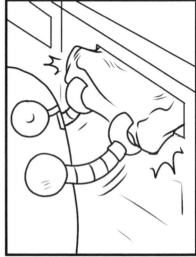

Say... The mail robot ought to be taught not to do that again!

Yes! We should give him a dressing down so he knows he nearly made mashed potatoes out of the parcel.

But wait a minute.... The robot was programmed to do this right? So, is it really the robot's fault?

What do YOU think?

The question is, will this change anytime soon?

"Ethical questions are the hardest to resolve because there are no clear-cut answers. And I certainly don't have the answer!" laughs Professor Ang with a twinkle in his eye. "But I would say that we are advancing in a good way by having robots help us with boring, dirty or dangerous tasks."

We're happy living in Singapore because our city is getting so clever, making our lives easier!

Smart City Singapore

Singapore is on track to becoming a smart city, aided by its autonomous robotic friends. In recent years, you may have seen some of these around Singapore: the driverless shuttle buses on the National University of Singapore's campus, the cleaning robot at Our Tampines Hub, the postal robot delivering mail in Punggol, or the ubiquitous tray-clearing robots at food courts in many malls.

Let's sCROOTinise!

Singapore is known to be a hyperconnected city. It is even seen to be the smartest city in the world by some. According to the IMD Smart City Index 2020, Singapore actually ranks first out of 109 cities in terms of being connected. With a long-term plan to become a fully Smart Nation, Singapore is currently transforming industries such as the health, transport, finance and education industries, with the help of AI and robotics.

Today, about 97% of Singapore's population can rely on high speed Internet in everyday life. This is great news for transforming the entire city into an even smarter one as we live more conveniently with AI-powered devices at our fingertips.

Together with AI that's been integrated into many aspects of daily life, robots are now increasingly used in Singapore. Some places you could run into robots in Singapore are schools, hospitals, factories, roads, housing estates, and community spaces like libraries and malls, and in homes.

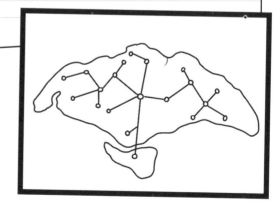

Professor Ang is happy to share that some of these helpful robots around town are made in his very own lab!

"We've been researching driverless autonomous vehicles (AVs), including cars, buses and even scooters for a while now. Seeing them on the roads, bringing people safely to and from their destinations, is a wonderful feeling!" Professor Ang shares enthusiastically, beaming as he speaks.

Here's Professor Ang with some of the self-driving vehicles that he has researched and created in his lab! We spy a bus, a car, a scooter... What else can you spot?

Photo credit: NUS Advanced Robotics Centre

Becoming a robot scientist

So, our robot-loving little friends, do you think Professor Ang has the dream job? We most certainly do!

How can you become a robot scientist just like Professor Ang and spend your days in your super special lab, working on bringing your dream robot to life?

Professor Ang's answer isn't what you may expect, like "Study harder" or "Go and complete your Maths homework". No, he's way cooler than that. (Although he does agree that you'll need to learn about computers and engineering to be good at making your robots work.)

Professor Ang and his students with a Kuka robotic arm they are researching. You most definitely need to know quite a bit about engineering and programming to understand how robots work!

Photo credit: NUS Advanced Robotics Centre

"One of the most important things you need to do if you want to be a robot scientist is to observe life. Find out how things work. Figure out what problems there are," says Professor Ang. "There are ALWAYS problems to be solved, and there are almost always answers to them. Then think about how robots can provide the solutions."

"Finally, think about how humans and robots can work together to solve these problems, great and small. Looking at robots as helpful partners and collaborators, not as threats, will unlock even greater potential for problem-solving."

Chapter 5

"You'll never have to mop your own floors again," they said...

Do you own any of these robots in your home?

If you think of robots in the home, what's the first image that comes to your mind? Do you picture personal butlers that follow you around, attending to your every whim and fancy? Robotic pets that provide company while your parents are out at work? Or a metallic helper in the kitchen to cook your meals for you?

Well, a few people actually HAVE these in their homes right now! But most people don't, because such robots still cost more than the world's most expensive potato – the La Bonnotte, which happens to cost about US$600 per kilogram!

What you may be more used to seeing are really cool devices like Google Home or Amazon's Alexa. These are virtual assistants powered by very clever artificial intelligence technology. From playing music to checking the weather, to typing and sending text messages, you only need to voice out your command with a "Hey Google!" and it's done, just like that... but are these robots?

If we're allowing robots into our homes, we've certainly come a long way from 200 years ago, when a group of fabric workers in the UK was so afraid that machines were stealing their jobs that they smashed them right up. Now, please don't go smashing your robot vacuums up! That would make Mum and Dad reaaaaallly mad!

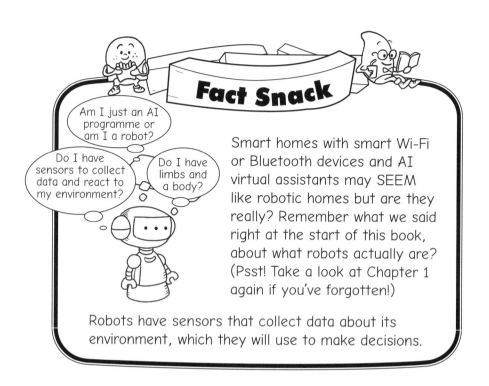

Fact Snack

Am I just an AI programme or am I a robot?

Do I have sensors to collect data and react to my environment?

Do I have limbs and a body?

Smart homes with smart Wi-Fi or Bluetooth devices and AI virtual assistants may SEEM like robotic homes but are they really? Remember what we said right at the start of this book, about what robots actually are? (Psst! Take a look at Chapter 1 again if you've forgotten!)

Robots have sensors that collect data about its environment, which they will use to make decisions.

So it is now official: Our homes are filled with smart machines and appliances, robots and non-robots alike. It is also a fact that many of our homes today have smart home virtual assistants like Google Assistant or Amazon Echo, with more than 126 million smart home assistants installed in US homes as of June 2021*. And while they are not robots, they are excellent at executing commands!

*according to a report by the Consumer Intelligence Research Partners.

Which of these are smart systems outfitted with artificial intelligence and which of these are robots? Take a guess!

1. The fridge that can tell you when you're out of cereal and milk

2. The alarm clock that runs away when you don't wake up so that you're forced to stand up to chase after it to shut it off

3. The smart vacuum and mop that can map out your house and clean every nook and cranny

4. The smart sound system that plays different songs the moment you ask it to

5. The kitchen help-mate with steel arms that can take ingredients off the shelf and pour them into the pan and cook everything at the same time

6. The curtains that automatically open at 7am every morning so you won't be late for school

I've been proudly vacuuming your home floors since 1996 and I'm now available with a mop function too!

Did you manage to get them all right?

Answers: 1) AI 2) Robot 3) Robot 4) AI 5) AI 6) AI

Cleaning robots: Can your floors be cleaned without you lifting a finger?

More than 14 million households in the United States alone can tell you loudly and proudly that the answer is YES!

Let's scROOTinise!

Robot vacuums are so smart at avoiding obstacles because they've got cameras and sensors that work hard to map the whole area out before they get down to cleaning. These maps are stored in their memory so that they know how big each room is and where its walls are. These same sensors also tell them when there's a random object they need to avoid or when there is a particularly dirty patch they need to pay attention to. When this happens, each robot can retrace its steps to clean up and make sure ALL the dirt's been sucked up!

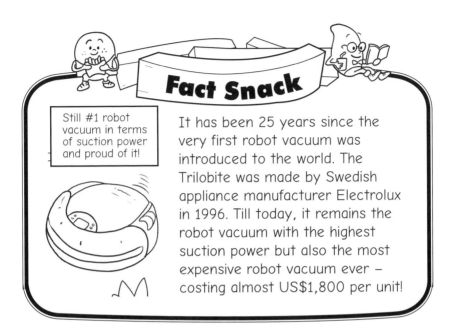

Fact Snack

Still #1 robot vacuum in terms of suction power and proud of it!

It has been 25 years since the very first robot vacuum was introduced to the world. The Trilobite was made by Swedish appliance manufacturer Electrolux in 1996. Till today, it remains the robot vacuum with the highest suction power but also the most expensive robot vacuum ever – costing almost US$1,800 per unit!

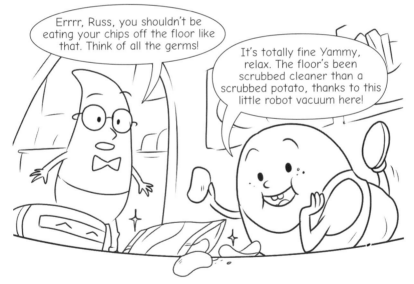

In fact, many robot vacuums come with an in-built mopping function too, so they leave your floors so clean you could eat potatoes right off them.

Kitchen robots

Say hello to your robot chef with actual robotic arms!

Smart kitchens may be everywhere now, with Wi-Fi-enabled appliances that relieve you of even pressing buttons! Good news for all you lazy potatoes out there. Also, there are appliances for almost every type of cooking you could need: the KitchenAid for baking, the Thermomix for cooking, as well as very efficient juicers and other aids...

But what about actual robots in the kitchen?

Spud the Bot

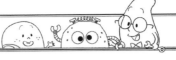

The Moley Robotic kitchen is a true-to-life robot chef made up of two robotic arms. It can replicate the hand movements of professional chefs that it has been taught by, and is able to cook from thousands of saved recipes, retrieve cut ingredients from a fridge, adjust stove temperatures, whisk and stir as the food is cooking, and plate it all up like a pro. It even washes up without complaining! One thing it can't do yet? Peel potatoes. PHEW!

Fact Snack

Robots that can help out in all areas of the house are being developed right now – can we hear a HOORAY? One such robot is Samsung's Bot Handy, a tall and skinny white-and-black robot that has a shoulder, an elbow and a wrist. It even has a pair of eyes that changes expression as it goes around! Bot Handy is being taught to do all sorts of things around the house, like pour a glass of milk, pick up laundry, and load the dishwasher. Maybe you could even teach it to do your homework for you?

Robot personal assistants

Robot assistants are really cool. Their largest cool factor? Helping you stay out of trouble with Mum and Dad by reminding you of chores you have to do before you get nagged at.

For some groups of people who need more help or support with their needs, robot assistants can even make a huge difference between life and death!

There are quite a few personal assistant robots out there these days, so you are quite spoilt for choice if you are looking to get one. Some of them have additional functions that even let them patrol your home while everyone is out. Talk about a super-powered personal assistant!

Some personal assistant robots that you can easily buy are the robots Aido, Alpha, Zenbo, Kuri, Buddy and Pillo.

Fact Snack

What makes these robots so helpful for old folks? Well, people tend to have poorer memories as they grow older and have more health complications. So, these personal assistant robots can be a great help in reminding our elderly loved ones at home to take their medicines. Pillo is one such robot. It also uses facial recognition to ensure that the right medication is dispensed to the right person, because taking the wrong medications could make something go SPUD-tacularly wrong!

Robot pets

Been trying for years to persuade Mum and Dad to get you a dog or cat but they keep saying no? This is one pet they may say yes to – a Robot Pet! These robotic pets are a new breed of bots designed for the sole purpose of being a companion without requiring the effort that goes into caring for a live pet. They can learn tricks, make sounds and they love being petted!

Fact Snack

Can people form real bonds with their robotic pets? You may think it unlikely but a study conducted by a university in the United States in the 2000s showed that children did form emotional attachments with their robotic Furby toys. Some researchers got the children to hold a guinea pig, a Furby and a Barbie doll upside down to see how the children would react to them. The children immediately righted the hamster when it began to squirm and the Furby after about 30 seconds when it began to tremble and say that it was scared. The children had no problems holding the Barbie dolls upside down for a long time and only turned the dolls back up when their hands got tired!

I am scared...
My eyes are
swirls now!

Spud the Bot

There're many robot pets that you can get these days, but the most famous one has to be Aibo. First developed by Sony in 1999, it's the ancestor of robotic pets today but has since learnt new tricks, thanks to software updates! This little robo-pup can make doggy sounds, play with toys and interact differently with individual members of the family, thanks to face recognition cameras. It can now also anticipate when you will come home and greet you at the door with pure doggy joy!

Scan this to see how Aibo behaves just like a real pup!

Spud the Bot

If you want a more realistic looking pet, you will want to keep your eyes peeled for the Moflin! It looks and behaves very much like a soft little guinea pig, and it even has an internal emotion map that gives each bot its own unique personality, which develops depending on its environment and how it is treated. It's being perfected in the labs right now and may one day be available in a store near you!

I'm furry, I'm cute, and the best part is I'll never die and you'll never have to cry!

Robots that help you relax

One of the best things to do at home has to be relaxing after a long day at school. These home robots take chilling at home to a higher level. They don't do your chores though, so you'll need one of those cleaning robots we mentioned earlier if you REALLY want to unplug and relax without anyone breathing down your neck...

Spud the Bot

Is your little brother suddenly not feeling like giving you a back massage in spite of your best efforts to bribe, threaten or beg him? You won't need to anymore with this handy massage robot: the iYu Pro Massage Robot made by Capsix Robotics. Its robotic arm is equipped with sensors and a camera. It also remembers lessons taught by human physiotherapists so that it massages you just right, leaving you in bliss and all ready for... another new week of school?

Ahhhhh, Russ, this is so good, thanks for the massage!

Don't mention it. It's small potatoes (to me)!

There's nothing quite like sinking into your couch and hugging a cushion tight to de-stress. Well, how about hugging a pillow robot?

Spud the Bot

Part pet and part cushion, the Qoobo is a fluffy cushion with a furry tail that resembles a cat. Say what?! It purrs, reacts to stroking, and randomly wags its tail when left alone for too long. It even comes in a petite version for your littlest siblings to cuddle!

Ahhhhh, there's plenty of cuddles for each of us with these fluffy, furry Qoobo robots.

Spud-dles for all!

Chapter 6

It's not all work and no play!

Playtime with robots

Robots don't need to play or be entertained, but that doesn't mean they can't entertain us! In fact, they are really good at doing just that. We can play games with them, watch them perform for us, or cheer them on at special competitions for robots! They also appear in movies and sporting events. Talk about being multi-talented!

Fact Snack

The ancestors of robots – automatons – were first made to entertain rich people. Automatons are exactly what you think they are: things that can operate by themselves, without needing people to move them.

There are many examples of these early automata recorded in ancient cultures all over the world: the Greeks made flying birds and cuckoo clocks, while a king in ancient China was presented with a life-sized humanoid automaton that could walk and move. It even had internal organs that were recreated and held together by leather, wood and glue.

Nonetheless, modern robots weren't built for entertainment. They were initially made to relieve workers of mundane or repetitive tasks, to make work more efficient. What's cool though is that these bots are so smart that they can learn things they weren't even made to do.

Coding robots I

Hey kids, listen up! You'll want to memorise these five magical letters "S-T-E-A-M", because these are the kinds of toys your parents will most definitely want you to be playing with! What is STEAM, you might ask? STEAM stands for science, technology, engineering, arts and mathematics. The most aPEELing news? Many toy robots are STEAM toys!

Robot toys these days can look like anything and everything – a cute ball with big eyes, a pretty doll, a dancing unicorn or a transforming car. You could even construct robot toys entirely from scratch using Lego or other parts, customise their builds and programme them to do things!

These programmable robots are known as **coding robots**.

One of the most well-known kits for coding robots is from Lego, which has been around since 1998.

Spud the Bot

The Lego Mindstorms Robot Inventor Kit will literally bring all your robot-building dreams to life. You can build up to five robots from the 949 pieces in the kit, and the robots can be programmed on a cool coding programme called Scratch* to do lots of awesome things according to their specific builds. One robot could blast its way through obstacles, while another could perfect a robotic slam dunk!

If you're good enough, you could even get your robot to enter the World Robot Olympiad, a competition for these robotic creations to see who's the best programmed among them all. See page 90 to find out more about these exciting games!

* Scratch is a coding language that children can use to create games, digital stories and animations. It features a simple visual interface that is easy for children to grasp.

Scan this QR code to have a look at the five robots you can build and what they can do!

Coding robots II

Spud the Bot

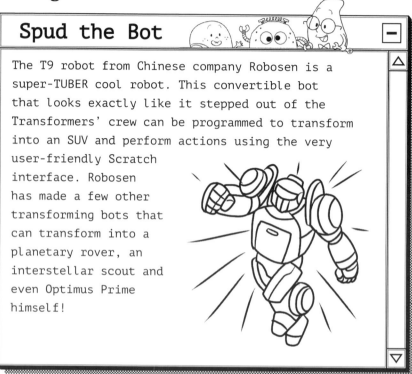

The T9 robot from Chinese company Robosen is a super-TUBER cool robot. This convertible bot that looks exactly like it stepped out of the Transformers' crew can be programmed to transform into an SUV and perform actions using the very user-friendly Scratch interface. Robosen has made a few other transforming bots that can transform into a planetary rover, an interstellar scout and even Optimus Prime himself!

Scan the QR code of the T9 robot to see it transform into an SUV!

Just like how there are potatoes of all sizes, there are coding robots for kids of all ages. That's right, your little sister or brother can work on their own robot without destroying your carefully built bot. Some of these robots are the Botley, Sphero and the Wonder Dash robot.

Fact Snack

Your younger sibling's coding robots may look cute, but these robots are excellent at teaching children useful things that adults love – like teamwork, problem solving, maths, engineering and critical thinking. Why? Because these robots guide children to think logically and express their instructions clearly to get their robot to do fun things, like dance, light up or move in certain directions, all while making it feel like a game!

Music robots

If you have heard that robots can do almost everything that humans can except create art and play music, this next category of robots will abso-ROOT-ly blow your mind! MUSIC ROBOTS. That's right, these bots can play music just like humans can.

Spud the Bot

Meet the metal band to rival all metal bands: Z Machines. This Japanese three-robot band is made up of a 78-fingered guitar-playing robot named Mach, a 22-armed drumming robot Ashura, and Cosmo, who plays the keyboard using lasers. Other than headlining the 2013 Maker Faire Tokyo convention, the trio have also collaborated with English electronica musician Squarepusher on his 2014 extended play EP record, titled very fittingly as "Music for Robots".

If you're wondering if having 78 fingers would help you to play the piano better, well, Beethoven and Mozart got on excellently having just 10!

Let's sCROOTinise!

These aren't exactly bots, but it's worth knowing that AI programmes in computers can write music of all kinds! The computers learn the patterns and structures of thousands of songs. Then, they generate new tunes and variations of lines based on what they have learned. **Amper** is one such smart platform, which was created to generate original music for commercial use in videos, advertisements and podcasts. Even non-musicians can make their own melodies by indicating criteria like mood and genre in the programme!

Robots in movies

When you think of robots in the movies, the first ones that may come to your mind are probably the cool transforming bots in *Transformers*, or the lovable droids in *Star Wars*. There's just something so endearing about a fully sentient robot that you can talk to, joke with, argue with and ultimately become friends with.

Fact Snack

The two iconic droids from the *Star Wars* movies, the adorable R2D2, along with the eye-catching golden tin humanoid bot C3PO, are arguably among the most famous robots in the history of movie robots. However, did you know that they aren't true robots at all in real life? There were multiple copies of each of these droids on the movie sets and some were worn by actors and stuntmen, while others were operated via remote control. If you want to get your hands on a real-life R2D2, you can! Sphero has made an R2D2 that allows you to explore the Star Wars universe via a cool holographic simulation, or watch *Star Wars* movies with it. It even beeps according to the script!

Other than being really good in movies, robots are now also involved in movie making. With their tirelessness and ability to zoom in and out of super-fast-moving subjects in a split second without missing a beat, robots have taken precision shooting to a whole new level!

This robot is faster and more flexible than I am! But that won't stop me from trying to beat it. Ouch!

You've got a muscle cramp now, right?

The Kira by Motorized Precision, a US-based company, is a special camera robot that gives filmmakers the ability to shoot scenes unbounded by human reaction time. It can be manoeuvred in multiple directions using an X-Box controller or have its route pre-programmed on a computer, and can move up to nine feet per second in any direction. That's way faster than you can yell "ALRIGHT, MUM!" when she tells you to pick your dirty laundry off the floor.

Scan the QR code to have a look at the Kira robot in action!

Robots in sports

Imagine seeing 11 robots on the soccer field taking on the best of the best in soccer in the world and beating them – that's what a group of robot scientists hope to achieve by the year 2050. Robots that can play soccer already exist, but the truth is that they're about as good as a bunch of preschoolers kicking a ball around for fun. There are also robots that can play basketball, table tennis, and even sumo wrestle! But none of them are very good at the sport they play yet.

Well, for as long as these sports robots retain their humanoid forms, roboticists are able to optimise their creations to outperform their human counterparts, for example, by creating a torpedo-shaped robot to outswim world champion, Michael Phelps. But where is the fun in that, eh? You may as well throw a potato with a motor into the pool and see how fast it can go. (The answer is: not very fast at all, since potatoes will get soggy quickly!)

Fact Snack

The World Robot Olympiad is a global competition for robots to compete in missions to see who comes up on top. First held in 2004 in Singapore, it has been held in different countries every year since then, including Thailand, China, Taiwan, Japan, South Korea, Philippines, United Arab Emirates, Malaysia, Indonesia, Russia, Qatar, India, Costa Rica, Hungary and Germany. Today, an incredible 80,000 young robot scientists from 85 different countries take part in the games!

Let's sCROOTinise!

Sporty bots are best deployed to help us humans get better at the sports we play. There are a few ways that robots can help us in this. One of the ways is to hone players' skills by acting as a robotic opponent. Today, top volleyball players in Japan are using one such robot, developed by researchers at the Japanese Volleyball Association and Tsubaka University, to train. It is a block machine with programmable arms that mimics the tactics and techniques of opponents so that players can perfect their attacks.

Tater Toons

Do you think if we went too near the robot, it'd mistake us for a volleyball and try to throw us?

I don't know, fellow potato, but let's not find out and stay clear of it!

Scan the QR code to see the volleyball robot in action!

Chapter 7

Welcome to your future, kids: meet your robotic teachers!

Learning with robots

Robots work and play with us, and they help us in our homes and hospitals. Little wonder that they can be found in our schools too! While robots aren't ready to take over classes on a day-to-day basis, they're playing an increasingly bigger role in your classrooms and school corridors as the years go by.

Fact Snack

Let's travel back in time to the year 1974 to meet the first robot teacher ever invented – the 90 kg-heavy, 180 cm-tall Leachim. Invented by Michael J Freeman to teach 4th graders in an elementary school in the Bronx, it was programmed with the curriculum, information of each student in the class, encyclopedia entries, an entire dictionary and loads of jokes. It could quiz students individually, even remembering their past scores, and direct them to the correct pages in their textbooks for the correct answers.

Unfortunately, Leachim was stolen from the back of a truck in 1975, so he couldn't continue his teaching career. The good news is that there are now new robots that do what he did and more in schools today.

Some things that robots do in schools today include making learning fun, marking, remote teaching and helping students with special needs learn better. More and more students are also learning the basics of robotics with the help of – you got it – robots!

Robot teachers

He's got a screen for his face and his body is a slim metal rod. Legs? Who needs legs when you've got wheels! Meet Mr Robot, the newest member of your school's staff of teachers. You may think you can fool Mr Robot into believing that you're paying attention when you're really snoozing at your desk, but Mr Robot's just as sharp as your regular human teacher (thanks to his many cameras and sensors!) and he may whizz over to dunk an ice cube on your head to wake you up.

While this may seem like fiction for now (as far as dumping ice on your face goes, anyway, at least not in schools!), robots have been in the classroom for quite a while now.

Fact Snack

Are robots more effective teachers than humans? While they certainly have better memories, they aren't as great at nurturing that important relationship between a student and teacher! Think about it, you probably wouldn't be able to turn to your robotic teacher for comfort if you're terrified about failing your upcoming exam, whereas your human teacher would certainly lend you a listening ear and share some nuggets of wisdom with you!

Let's sCROOTinise!

A school in Bengaluru, India has a humanoid robot named Eagle 2.0 in the classrooms, imparting subject knowledge and even answering questions from 300 students daily. Though dressed in human clothes and sporting long brown hair, Eagle 2.0 isn't meant to take the place of the human teacher. She assists the teacher in the classroom by delivering fixed content while the teacher focuses on mentoring the kids, providing emotional support and teaching them problem solving. She currently teaches five subjects: Physics, Chemistry, Biology, Geography and History. The coolest thing? This robot was 3D printed, assembled and programmed by a team of 17 really smart members of staff from the school!

Some other countries that have robots teaching in schools are Finland, China, Korea and Japan. Have YOU seen robots teaching in schools in your country yet?

Learning robotics in school

The first robotics programme for children was introduced in the 1980s in just a handful of schools in the United States.

Since then, more and more robotics programmes have been introduced in schools all over the world in the form of elective programmes and courses. Think about it: your school probably has a Robotics Club, or perhaps your parents have signed you up for a robotics camp before?

Have you ever wondered what you could learn in a robotics class? Let's find out!

Lego Mindstorms is one of the most widely used learning robots in the world. (Head back to page 81 to find out more about this exceptionally cool Lego set that's way more than a toy!) In the United States alone, half of all middle schools and about a quarter of all elementary and high schools are using Lego Mindstorms in their teaching curriculum.

Mindstorms is awesome at teaching robotics because it lets you explore your creativity by building virtually anything you can imagine, with the nifty additions of sensors, motors and microprocessors, to bring your colourful Lego creations to robotic life. You could literally build a Lego triceratops that can avoid walls as it walks around in less than 20 minutes. In fact, you probably need more time than this just to finish your Maths homework.

Educational robots

Remember those coding robots we talked about in Chapter 6? Well, these bots we're going to talk about next are great educational companions too! Yes, they make even better educational companions than potatoes do. They teach you super complex skills like programming and logical sequencing – the basic skills needed to programme a robot – in a way that makes it all seem like a fun game.

There are other educational robots that teach languages and other subjects. The Nao robot is one such educational robot. It is a humanoid robot created by SoftBank Robotics and is programmable for customised education and research purposes. Since 2015, more than 5,000 Nao robots are currently being used in schools and laboratories in over 50 countries across the world.

Spud the Bot

Robin, the Nao robot, was part of a European project to teach young children a second language with the help of social robots. Between 2016 and 2018, Robin taught 208 Dutch kids between the ages of four to six the English language by giving them one-on-one lessons disguised as short simple games. The children managed to learn about 34 new words from Robin during his stint teaching them - that's a wonderful start for first-time robot teachers!

Pick one of the following to classify a potato. A - a root vegetable, B - a fruit, C - a seed.

I'll go with A - a root vegetable. I'm a potato. If I don't know this, I wouldn't be able to live it down.

Some robotic games can teach useful things such as:

1.   Language

2.   Maths concepts

3.   Memory skills

4.   Social skills

Well actually, if you think about it, robots can teach almost ANYTHING. They're that awesome.

Robots for remote learning

How many home-based learning days have you had lately? During the global COVID-19 pandemic, the idea of remote school became more common for many people.

For some of us, attending lessons from home may be as simple as going online, doing our homework, completing it and hitting "submit". Or attending a virtual class with our teachers and friends over a video call.

For some others, remote learning also includes the presence of a friendly robot. These robots have microphones and speakers, and they follow actions and sounds in the classrooms closely. Students who are attending classes from home can also interact with their classmates in the classroom. All these help to make the student feel like he's right there in class too, staying closely connected with what's going on in school despite being miles away at home.

Sounds amazing? Totally! And it's happening in classrooms around the world today. One such classroom it's happening in is an elementary school in Washington, where robots such as Swivl are changing the way students experience a classroom lesson from the comforts of their own home.

Swivl looks like a simple tablet holder, but remember the saying: "Don't let appearances fool you." This neat little robot with an inbuilt camera, speaker and microphone is able to nimbly swivel around to track a person or object with the help of an infrared marker.

What this means is that it can perfectly track a teacher holding on to the marker, and it captures her voice and movement clearly and precisely. If you were the student sitting at home, you could talk to your teacher with ease as she walks around the classroom, all the while with the helpful robot following her around and providing the unique up-close-and-personal perspective. It would almost feel like you were there in person, following her around the classroom yourself!

Scan this QR code to feel what it is like to be a student attending a class from home with the help of Swivl!

Fact Snack

Robots in the classroom are only going to become more common — yes, you heard it here first! With more schools adopting hybrid modes of learning that includes classroom days and home-based learning days, it's only natural that robots will become a greater part of your school life. Robots, together with smart tools like interactive whiteboards, pens that scan text straight from the book to the screen, tablets and laptops (collectively known as the Internet of Things), are set to change the way you learn, for the better. Are you ready?

Robots to help students with learning disabilities

One of the best things about educational robots is that they have the superpower of helping children with special needs learn a whole lot better. Not every child learns the same way, and robots are able to provide personalised help.

Kids with autism and other learning needs may need help with some basic tasks that are often taken for granted, like social greetings and behaviour, understanding instructions, or keeping focus. With educational robots around, these kids will get the personalised help they need in the company of a non-judgemental, friendly companion. That's great news, isn't it?

Fact Snack

Robots make such smashing learning companions for children with special learning needs because for many of these children, human interactions are difficult. They often feel more comfortable around non-human objects.

When these children were placed in a learning session with both a robot and a person, it was discovered that the kids spent twice as much time looking at the robot and yet, displayed only half the repetitive behaviours (a sign of anxiety) as compared to when they attended a session with a human person.

Spud the Bot

In an elementary school in South Carolina, a little boy who is about 10 years old is exchanging standard greetings with a robot named Milo. Milo waves at him, and when the boy reaches out his hand to touch Milo, Milo prompts him: "Say hi to Milo". A normal exchange of greetings is tough for this little boy because he is a child with autism and is unable to respond appropriately in social situations.

Milo the robot can help these children practise the correct behaviours. It's a clever robot that can show human expressions on its face, teaching the kids how to identify facial cues and also respond to the children's voices and actions.

Hi robot! How are you feeling?

I'm just a potato and no expert in human emotions, but I would guess you look pretty pleased?

Yes, you are right. I am showing my pleased face!

Scan the QR code to see Milo working with a child with autism on how to identify human facial expressions!

Other robots help children with special learning needs by practising expected behaviours and reactions with them. For instance, a Leka robot that is thrown on the floor or hit will show a sad facial expression. This shows the child that her act of throwing or hitting Leka makes it sad and teaches her not to do it again.

Robots are truly doing some SPUD-tacular work as learning aides and educational helpers. While it's unlikely that robots will ever fully take the place of human teachers in the classrooms, don't you think they make absolutely wonderful additions to the learning experience?

Chapter 8

They'll go where we cannot, to be our eyes, hands and feet

Robots going where we cannot

There are many places on Earth that have yet to be properly explored. In fact, around 65 percent of Earth falls into this category! Actually, that's great news! There's still lots of the world for us to uncover!

What this also means is that most of the places that are left to discover are places that are hard to reach.

There are some conditions our bodies are unable to withstand, or places we may have great difficulty visiting, as much as we would love to. So our visits to these places may be limited and require lots of planning beforehand. Some of such places are tiny deep sea caves, bitter cold ice lakes, scorching hot deserts, extremely dangerous radioactive wastelands, and even outer space.

Well, the good news is that there are robots that can make these exploration trips for us without even the slightest fuss.

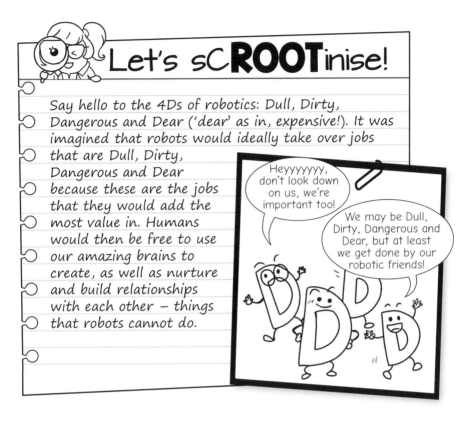

Let's sC**ROOT**inise!

Say hello to the 4Ds of robotics: Dull, Dirty, Dangerous and Dear ('dear' as in, expensive!). It was imagined that robots would ideally take over jobs that are Dull, Dirty, Dangerous and Dear because these are the jobs that they would add the most value in. Humans would then be free to use our amazing brains to create, as well as nurture and build relationships with each other – things that robots cannot do.

Heyyyyyyy, don't look down on us, we're important too!

We may be Dull, Dirty, Dangerous and Dear, but at least we get done by our robotic friends!

Robots exploring some of the most dangerous places on Earth and beyond certainly falls into the Dangerous category!

Let's have a look at some hair-raising and eye-popping places that robots are exploring for us. Who knows, maybe one day we'll get to go to these places too! But with robots doing some of the legwork, gathering useful data and images for us before we embark on these journeys ourselves, we daresay the journey may just be a little bit easier on us.

Tater Toons

Robots exploring what's under our feet

Ever wondered what the ground under our feet looks like? Perhaps you've not given much thought to it, but a group of people have been doing lots and lots of research to see if it's at all possible to live underground.

(Potatoes live underground too, but that's another story for another time!)

The hardest thing about all this is that exploring underground is hard, hard work – even with the right protective gear. For one thing, can you imagine breathing in the soil with the particles going into your nostrils, eyes and mouth?

Say hello to underground robots, a special breed of robots created just for exploring the vast world below our feet.

You may think that big chunky robots would be more effective at making their way around down below, with so much sand to dig through. Think again. One of the most effective underground bots today are burrowing bots that look very much like wriggly earthworms. Thanks, Mother Nature, for the idea! These soft, wormy bots are absolute pros at shovelling dirt away. They are filled with a special fluid that helps them move like worms and are equipped with sensors to help them move and tunnel into just the right places.

Some of the underground environments we have yet to explore adequately are underground caves and tunnels. They're dark, narrow, filled with water and altogether extremely difficult for humans to explore safely.

Robots are currently being used by miners to map out mines and gather valuable information about the types of rocks and minerals within. Robots are also helping miners see beyond flooded tunnels – something that would be dangerous for humans to accomplish.

Such cave robots are able to walk, climb, swim and even fly in tight spaces. That's no mean feat, even for a robot!

Scan the QR code to see a drone flying by itself in a dark cave.

Robots exploring jungles

Jungles and rainforests are home to thousands of species of creatures – many of them have never even been discovered yet. As excited as you are to hear this, it's probably not a great idea to jump right into your nearest rainforest in the name of exploration without proper preparation. There are lots you'll need to pack, such as weeks and weeks of food and water supplies, as well as poison antidotes and medications. Imagine how much stuff you'll have to lug around!

It's going to take more than a poisoned hamburger to take me down...

Robots don't get hungry and are unaffected by poison though, so they make the perfect explorers!

That's precisely what rainforest scientists have been turning to lately, with new robotics projects in the works to deploy robots to study jungles like the Amazon rainforest and its biodiversity.

Spud the Bot

Robotics firm Data61 has been monitoring the Amazon rainforest with the help of scientists, a wireless network of sensors, and soon, mobile robots.
Drawing inspiration from the ants that crawl along the floor of the rainforest, the resident robot that will be prowling around the dense jungle ground of the Amazon is named Weaver. With six legs like an ant and smart sensors all around, it crawls

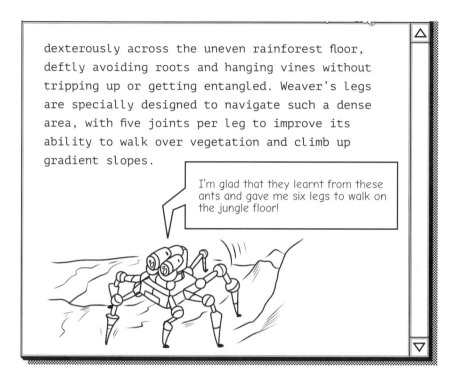

dexterously across the uneven rainforest floor, deftly avoiding roots and hanging vines without tripping up or getting entangled. Weaver's legs are specially designed to navigate such a dense area, with five joints per leg to improve its ability to walk over vegetation and climb up gradient slopes.

I'm glad that they learnt from these ants and gave me six legs to walk on the jungle floor!

Robots exploring radioactive sites

Imagine a blast so deadly that it can wipe out an entire city like Singapore just like that, turning everything into dust and ashes. This can actually happen in the event of a nuclear explosion. What's even worse is that it also has other damaging effects that last a long time.

A nuclear explosion always results in a nuclear fallout, which is the release of radioactive materials into the air. This is extremely dangerous. Here's why, and we'll try to keep it quick.

Radioactive materials release energy that has harmful effects on people and the environment, and they stay on for years and years. These particles get onto everything that's around the explosion – yes, we really mean everything.

They settle onto the surfaces of the things and plants that are left, seep into the ground, and dissolve into water bodies like rivers and oceans. They even get stuck in the clouds, later falling back to earth as radioactive rain!

Because radioactive particles can mess up your body's cells and tissues, people who are exposed to the nuclear fallout, or who live on or close to the sites of nuclear explosions can get really sick – even years after the actual incident.

The effects of a nuclear fallout are also found in the wake of what is called a nuclear meltdown. Nuclear meltdowns are what happen when something goes terribly wrong in a nuclear power plant, and a reactor (a part of the energy-generating system) is damaged due to overheating.

One of the most significant nuclear accidents in recent history happened in 2011, in Fukushima in Japan, where the flooding of the lower parts of four of the plant's reactors by a tsunami resulted in three meltdowns and radiation leak into the surrounding waters and town. Another famous nuclear accident that took place was in the Russian town of Chernobyl in 1986.

Years may have passed but it's still dangerous for humans to be near the reactors today. So thank goodness for special robots that have been sent in to have a look at what's going on, collect data and clean up.

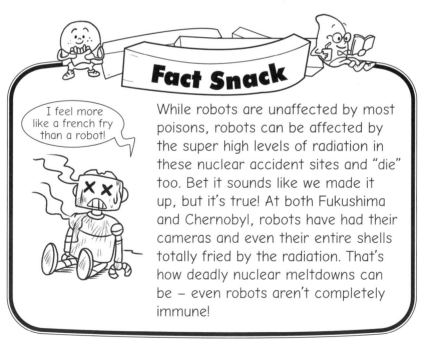

Fact Snack

I feel more like a french fry than a robot!

While robots are unaffected by most poisons, robots can be affected by the super high levels of radiation in these nuclear accident sites and "die" too. Bet it sounds like we made it up, but it's true! At both Fukushima and Chernobyl, robots have had their cameras and even their entire shells totally fried by the radiation. That's how deadly nuclear meltdowns can be – even robots aren't completely immune!

Little Sunfish is a unique robot that has been built specifically to aid the efforts at Fukushima. It can swim underwater in complete darkness and withstand huge amounts of radiation without getting its chipset or cameras short-circuited. This innocuous-looking little robot the size of a loaf of bread is equipped with sensors and cameras at its front and back, and has five propellers. Its mission is like that of many others before it - to locate the melted nuclear fuel so that the plant can eventually be decommissioned and hopefully cleaned up! It did actually locate the melted nuclear fuel on its second trip into the reactor so we're definitely taking baby steps towards cleaning the Fukushima nuclear plant up!

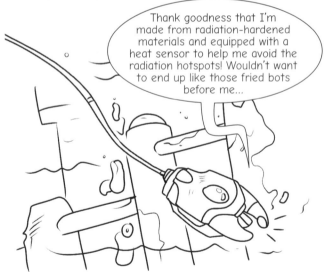

Thank goodness that I'm made from radiation-hardened materials and equipped with a heat sensor to help me avoid the radiation hotspots! Wouldn't want to end up like those fried bots before me...

Robots exploring space

It's not a secret that robots have been sent to space for a while now. With all the unknowns, robots are truly perfect for the job.

Are you wondering what kind of robots are helping us with our space exploration? Well, all kinds! From rovers to satellites to space probes, to humanoid robots and little hovering cube personal assistants, robots are truly doing a fantastic job assisting humans in our gargantuan quest of space exploration.

The very first space robots were very simple robotic satellites that were only equipped with a radio transmitter powered by batteries. Today, there are robotic arms that can repair satellites and other spacecraft, as well as rovers that can explore a totally different planet like Mars (we'll talk about one such rover in just a moment).

Space robots are really, really cool, and we have them to thank for much of what we know about space and all its hidden mysteries. You could even say that robots have made the impossible possible.

The very first robot that was sent to space was the Sputnik 1, in 1947, by the then Union of Soviet Socialist Republics (USSR). It was just a simple probe that looked a lot like a silver basketball. Sputnik 1 orbited Earth for three weeks, sending radio signals back before its batteries went flat. While its mission in space was a brief one, Sputnik 1 paved the way for other more advanced robots to make their way to space by providing scientists with the data needed to calculate important things, like the density of the upper atmosphere. Scan the QR code below to learn more about Sputnik 1's orbit around Earth for the very first time in history.

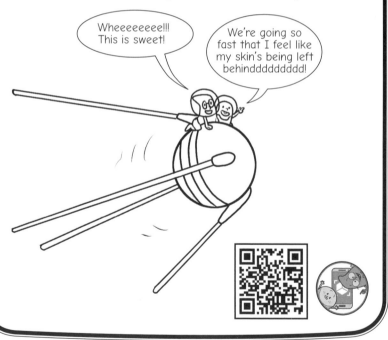

Spud the Bot

Perseverance is one of the most well-known space robots in the world - it's a little car-sized rover with six wheels, a robotic arm and a drill, and it's been rolling all over the Red Planet, Mars. You may even have seen videos of its landing on the dusty terrain of Mars on 18 February 2021, together with its friend, Ingenuity the robotic helicopter. It is currently searching for old life on Mars by collecting soil and rock samples and taking lots of pictures for scientists to analyse.

Built by the engineers and scientists at NASA's Jet Propulsion Laboratory in California, Perseverance joins fellow robotic rover Curiosity in its exploration of Mars. The two rovers have different missions though: Perseverance is hunting for signs of life while Curiosity is assessing the habitability of the Martian environment in the hopes that humans can someday live on Mars.

Scan the QR code below to see actual footage of the Perseverance rover landing on Mars!

Space robots through the years

From the battery-operated Sputnik to the multitude of robots working together on the International Space Station (ISS) today, you could say that space robots have come a long way. Today, the robots zipping around the solar system and beyond have abilities that are rather impressive.

You've already read about the Perseverance rover, the self-driving rover making its way around Mars as it looks very hard for signs of life on the red, dusty planet.

Now, let's have a look at more space robots through the years. From just one trip around Earth to galaxies beyond our very own Milky Way, you'll want to sit tight because this is going to be an out-of-this-world ride!

1. 1947 – Sputnik
The very first robot to orbit Earth.

2. 1966 – Surveyor rovers
These were the first seven robotic rovers to land on the moon, and they're all still there. They were able to quite cleverly make corrections to their flight mid-way and helped assess the softness and depth of the soil for the historic Apollo landing in 1969.

3. 1970 – Venera 7

This was the first unmanned robotic probe to land on another planet. Specifically, it landed on Venus.

4. 1977 – Voyager 1 & 2

These were the first unmanned robotic spacecrafts to visit Jupiter, Saturn, Uranus and Neptune. They are now in deep space, measuring the particle and magnetic properties of interstellar space.

5. 2004 – Rosetta Spacecraft

This was the first autonomous spacecraft to land on a comet and find out more about its nucleus. It's currently in deep space.

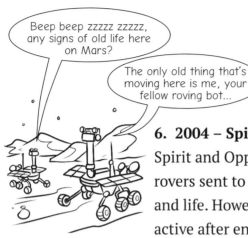

6. 2004 – Spirit and Opportunity

Spirit and Opportunity were robotic Mars rovers sent to look for old signs of water and life. However, the two are no longer active after encountering a sand trap and a dust storm on the Martian planet.

7. 2007 – Dawn Spacecraft

This was the first robotic spacecraft to investigate the giant protoplanet Vesta and dwarf planet Ceres. It's currently orbiting Ceres.

8. 2020 – Perseverance Rover

This is the latest robotic rover on Mars, hunting for signs of current life on the red planet. It's accompanied by Ingenuity, the very first robotic drone helicopter to fly on Mars.

9. Ongoing: 1998 to now – The International Space Station (ISS)

The ISS launched its very first component in 1998 and has been adding modules over the years. The latest pressurised module, Nauka, was just added in 2021. It's a multi-purpose laboratory that's part of the Russian segment of the ISS that will help its astronauts conduct even more research and experiments.

The ISS is the most complicated spaceship that exists today. Many out-of-this-world robots work on the ISS, helping human astronauts with their tasks big and small. From repairing spacecraft in space to helping the astronauts with their routine duties like inventory-taking, these robots make it possible for humans to live and work for prolonged periods in outer space.

There are robotic arms, a trio of flying cubes, and even a floating brain slated to join the motley crew!

Chapter 9
Robots of the future

What will robots of the future be like?

Robots are fast, precise and they can help us with so much. They can also help us extend our limitations, pushing the envelope to make the impossible possible.

As the past eight chapters have shown, there are robots helping us in every single sphere of our lives now. And with robots already exploring the final frontier of space even, is there anything new for robots to do in the future?

Not to worry, dear friends. There's still plenty for robots to do!

Let's get to the root of this and figure out what's in store in the future for these useful bots. Will they be all-present mega juggernauts that will stop at nothing to achieve their goals efficiently?

Or will they be the perfect friendly helpers, working SPUD-tacularly alongside us humans peacefully while we solve our problems, hand-in-hand?

While we cannot be 100 percent certain, we have a good feeling that the robots of the future won't be a nasty bunch at all. After all, the robots we know today are helping us greatly with our tasks in our homes, workplaces, schools, hospitals and community spaces.

And the question to ask ourselves is: "Do I feel threatened by the bots I see around me?"

For most of us, the answer would be a "no".

But will it really be okay when the robots take over some of our jobs for good? What do you think?

Robot takeover

The future will see some of our jobs being taken over by robots. In fact, some economists think that robots could take over 20 million manufacturing jobs all over the world by the year 2030. That's about the number of people in entire countries like Malawi or Syria!

Jobs that robots will take over

Sit tight when we say this because it's a shocker that you probably don't want to hear: robots ARE going to take some of our jobs.

Wait, what? Weren't we assured by Professor Ang in Chapter 4 that robots would be friendly?

Whoa whoa whoa, chill! Robots are going to take some of our jobs, but it will be totally fine. Yes, everything is going to be a-OK.

That's because they will be taking over jobs we DON'T WANT to do. Jobs that are – that's right, the 4Ds we mentioned in Chapter 8 – Dull, Dirty, Dangerous and Dear.

Manufacturing jobs do fall under those categories, especially because they are rather repetitive. Such jobs wouldn't benefit from having smart humans like us do them, and in fact, would be done better by robots that do not tire out and do not get bored.

And as it turns out, robots work best when working alongside humans.

In such a scenario, it's a win-win for everyone. The robots do the jobs that humans don't value-add much to, while humans focus on better work that only humans with our super special brains can excel at.

Now that we know that, what kinds of jobs do you think will be taken over by robots for good, and which jobs will be nearly impossible to be done by robots?

Look at the list below and take a guess which jobs will face a robotic takeover. Put a "yes"' next to them. And, put a "no" next to the jobs that you think will remain a human-only job forever.

1. Farmer

2. Customer service officer

3. Deliveryman

4. Supermarket shelf packer

5. Cleaner

6. Doctor

7. Teacher

8. Receptionist

9. Writer

10. Chef

11. Personal assistant

12. Bus driver

1. Yes 2. Yes 3. Yes 4. Yes 5. Yes 6. No 7. No 8. Yes 9. No 10. No 11. Yes 12. Yes

We don't have a crystal ball to show us the future (though we do have plenty of potato spud balls), but we do agree with smart scientists when they think that any job that is rote enough can be passed on to robots to relieve people from mundane, repetitive tasks. After all, the word "robot" comes from the Czech word "robota", which means "hard work", as we saw right at the start of this book in Chapter 1 – so robots are doing precisely the kind of work they are made to do!

Would you be surprised to hear that robots can learn new skills without needing to be programmed to do a task? You must be thinking, "What? You mean, robots have brains?" Yes, sort of. Some robots have artificial brains that even have neurons (in other words, their decision-making structures mimic the human brain). These artificial brains allow the robots to do something really cool known as Deep Learning and make decisions without human intervention.

Some robots are already capable of Deep Learning, but most of them are only capable of simpler Machine Learning.

Fact Snack

Machine Learning and Deep Learning are two terms that you will hear plenty of when people talk about robots and artificial intelligence (also known as AI).

 Tater Toons

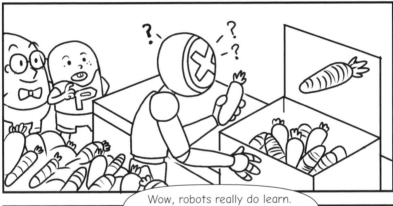

Let's sC**ROOT**inise!

The difference between Machine and Deep Learning is in the layer of learning the robot is able to process. A normal computer or machine works by following commands, or algorithms, that tell it what to do. This directed form of learning is Machine Learning. It happens when the computer system of a robot can learn something over time, but it usually requires direct instructions or input from a human. After some time and with enough direction, the computer learns.

Deep Learning is a more complicated type of Machine Learning that uses much more data, often without direct instructions from humans on what the data contains. The machine figures that out on its own. (Wow and double wow!) The robot essentially makes its decisions within an intelligent structure that you can think of as the brain of a robot – known as an artificial neural network.

Am I glad that this bot can take some of the heat off me when it comes to making decisions about choosing the right potatoes for the recipes!

To break it down even more fully, this image shows you the different levels of robotic intelligence.

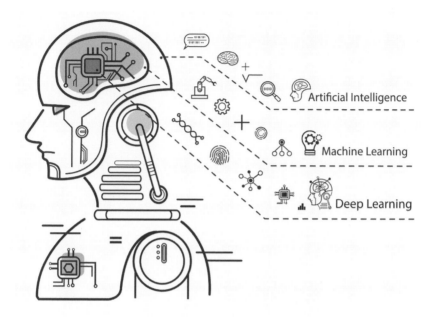

All robots possess **Artificial Intelligence** (AI), which is the ability to mimic human behaviour well. Some robots are able to undergo **Machine Learning**, which is a form of AI that allows it to learn something over time with the help of direct instructions from a human. Even fewer robots are able to undergo **Deep Learning**, which is a more sophisticated form of Machine Learning that enables the robot to make decisions on its own after repeated learning has been etched in its artificial neural network.

So more robots of the future will be able to undergo Deep Learning, to take on more complicated tasks and help us humans (and potatoes, hopefully!) improve our lives.

Robotic predictions

Robots that can learn – that sounds positively great, right? But, what will they look like?

For the most part, they will probably look a lot like what we are used to today.

But what could they be like exactly? Experts believe that these are some of the robots you are likely to see more of in the future:

1. Cobots

Cobots, short for Collaborative Robots, are going to be common because of the way we, as a society, are adapting to embracing robots in our midst. Robots aren't the enemy, not at all! They're here to help and work alongside us.

Cobots are designed to require direct human interaction to function. They are not going to replace humans; they will enhance the work that humans do and relieve certain demanding aspects of the job.

Fact Snack

Cobots today still look very much like an industrial robotic arm, only smaller and more lightweight. This makes them safe for humans to work with. Cobots are becoming more popular because they really do make industrial work easier on humans.

In 2019, there were more than 22,000 new cobots deployed in factories all over the world – that means 22,000 people received some welcome help from these helpful cobots!

Are you ready to work with a cobot when you're old enough to start work?

Scan the QR code to see cobots in action!

2. Nanobots

We explored this briefly in Chapter 3, but the fact of the matter is that nanobots aren't exactly big yet. (Well, of course they can't literally be big. They're called nanobots because of how tiny they physically are, but they're not popular yet – though they may be someday!)

They're mainly being developed for use in medicine. Soon, these powerful little robots will be able to monitor chronic illnesses such as diabetes and treat cancer as well as illnesses affecting sensitive areas, like the nervous system. Nanobots may someday even have the superpower to repair damaged cells and tissues!

Scan the QR code to have a look at how superpowered these miniscule nanobots are! Are you excited at their potential to cure more sick people or worried that they'll be used by bad people to harm us?

3. Autonomous vehicles

We talked about them in Chapter 2, so you know they're zipping around already. You may probably even have

taken a driverless train recently. What about driverless cars though? Well, they're on the rise for sure, and you can expect to see more of them on the roads real soon.

Tesla's driving AI system is becoming more and more sophisticated, while Hyundai's driverless taxi cars (Level 4, no less! If you forgot what Level 4 means, go back to Chapter 2 to find out!) are slated to be ready for commercial use sometime in 2023.

Scan this image to see this lady's first-hand experience of sitting in a driverless taxi in Shenzhen, China!

4. Soft robots

As robots become more advanced and are designed to do more out-of-this-world things, they should get tougher, right? Well, yes and no. Some robots are going to get softer.

Soft robots are super-duper flexible and can squeeze into tighter, twistier spaces than their harder counterparts can. They are also safer for humans to interact with – you won't need to worry about a heavy robot smacking you silly in the head.

Here are some soft robots that look like their animal counterparts. Take a guess as to what they resemble!

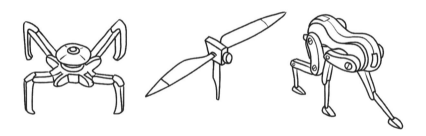

In what may seem like a happy coincidence, soft medical nanobots are currently being developed as we speak! These robots are designed to be controlled by magnets inside your nervous system to deliver drugs at extremely precise points within the spindly neural network.

Let's sC**ROOT**inise!

As their name suggests, soft robots are made from soft and elastic materials like silicone. They can move smoothly and are also extremely versatile, being both flexible in design and flexible in their function — very cool stuff, huh?

Their design draws lots of inspiration from living things like humans, animals, plants — and yes, even potatoes.

One of the challenges that roboticists face when designing soft robots is in making them strong. How's that going? Well, roboticists in MIT and Harvard have come up with a way of integrating an origami skeleton with a soft robot that resembles a human muscle, giving these bots the strength to lift something about 1,000 times their weight. That's definitely more than what we could lift, since most people can't even lift an object of our own weight!

Scan the QR code to have a look at other amazing soft robots at work!

5. Internet of Robotic Things

The Internet of Things. Have you heard of this phrase? If you haven't, now's a good time to listen up!

Fact Snack

The Internet of Things

Chances are, you're already acquainted with it. Do you have any things in your home that can be connected to the Internet? Things like your TV, the refrigerator, your watch or Google Assistant? Well, we're just getting started because more and more everyday things can connect to the Internet via Wi-Fi.

You can connect your morning alarm to the coffee machine and smart window blinds so all these things are done for you without you needing to lift a finger! Or, your smart fridge keeps an inventory and when items run out, the fridge's AI sends a shopping order via the grocery app on your phone and all you have to do is press "OK"!

While this may seem perfectly normal to us today, things weren't always like this. In fact, there was a time before the Internet existed. (Ask your parents!)

The Internet of Robotic Things takes us many steps closer towards an integrated smart world. That's because robots are going to get online and work together. Right now, there are industrial robots that are able to do this, making for an even more seamless workflow at the factories involved. Are you ready for labels that say "100% robot-made" in the future?

Scan the QR code to see robots working collaboratively with each other!

The End

So kids, do you now think that robots are even cooler than you thought they could be? The possibilities are limitless, way more than we can see, even with all the eyes we have as potatoes!

As they become more widespread, robots are going to be friendlier, safer and more collaborative than ever. They're here to help us in a big way and definitely here to stay. Robots are going to be really clever and helpful, and the future looks bright and SPUD-tacular!!

Science, Technology, Engineering and Maths (commonly known as STEM) are everywhere around us – look carefully and you'll see many examples.

Science Everywhere! is a fun series of books focusing on STEM concepts, and these books come with a huge dollop of corny humour!
Each book will enthrall young readers with the laugh-out-loud antics of potato detective duo, Yammy and Russ, who promise a mashing good time as they dig into the world of science.

WS Education

To receive updates about children's titles from WS Education, go to https://www.worldscientific.com/page/newsletter/subscribe, choose "Education", click on "Children's Books" and key in your email address.

Follow us @worldscienticedu on instagram and @World Scientific Education on YouTube for our latest releases, videos and promotions.